Original title:
Banana Blossoms

Copyright © 2025 Creative Arts Management OÜ
All rights reserved.

Author: Theodore Sinclair
ISBN HARDBACK: 978-1-80586-240-6
ISBN PAPERBACK: 978-1-80586-712-8

The Golden Heart of Summer

In the garden, a crown so bright,
With petals that giggle in morning light,
They sway in the breeze, oh what a sight,
Waving hello, with all their might.

A bunch of surprises, all stacked in a row,
Dancing to tunes only they seem to know,
They whisper sweet secrets, but never show,
What dreams hide inside, or where they will go.

Beneath the big leaf, they plot and they scheme,
Catching the sun in a golden beam,
With each little poke, they all scream and beam,
Life in their world is a whimsical dream.

So come take a peek at this sight oh so rare,
Where giggles and chuckles float in the air,
With laughter and joy, they dance without care,
In the heart of summer, a jolly affair.

Beneath the Canopy's Embrace

Under leafy hats so wide,
The laughter of blooms does hide.
Fruits in waiting, what a sight,
Swinging gently, pure delight.

In the shadows, secrets play,
Buzzing bees join in the fray.
With a giggle, petals sway,
Tickled by the light of day.

Secrets Unfold in Petal Layers

Layers of pink, gold, and green,
Hiding wonders, sights unseen.
Peeking out with cheeky grace,
Nature's jesters, time and space.

Whispers told in colors bright,
Revealing joy in soft twilight.
Ticklish thoughts in velvet folds,
Stories of the brave and bold.

The Fruitful Journey of Nature

On a whimsical, winding path,
Silly fruits are full of math.
Counting stars and spinning round,
In the orchard, joy is found.

Laughing leaves in a playful dance,
What a funny, silly chance.
To be merry, to be free,
Nature's shout, come play with me!

Sun-Kissed Monarchs of the Garden

Royal robes in golden hue,
Dancing light, a vibrant crew.
With a wink and charming flair,
They spread giggles through the air.

Ruling realms of sweet delight,
Wings unfurl, oh what a sight!
In this kingdom, laughter reigns,
Joyous hearts and sunny stains.

Touching the Silk of Eden

In the garden, a curious sight,
A cluster blooms, oh what delight!
Petals draping like a gown,
Whispers giggle, nature's clown.

They sway and dance in the warm air,
Droplets of nectar, oh what a flair!
Bumbles buzz around in glee,
What a party, come join me!

Mellow Hues Against the Sky

Underneath the sunny beams,
They glisten bright, like sculptured dreams.
With floppy hats, they take a stand,
Cheering on the frolic band.

Silliness splashes, as breezes play,
Swirling colors in a cabaret.
Come take a peek, the laughter spills,
In this spectacle, joy it fills!

Echoes of Lush Abundance

A whisper from the gardens' roast,
A party's here, let's raise a toast!
With every plume unfurling wide,
Even ants can't help but glide.

The playful critters join the show,
Twirling in a merry flow.
Nature's laughter fills the air,
With funny quirks, we can't compare!

Petals in a Golden Veil

Wrap me tight in soft embrace,
Each twist and turn, a silly chase.
Colors bright like summer's kiss,
A dance of whimsy, pure, and bliss.

As twilight drapes in dreamy hues,
They flutter on in playful views.
Who knew such magic could unfold,
In blooms so bright, and hearts so bold?

Underneath the Golden Canopy

Underneath the leafy shade,
A bunch of laughter softly swayed.
With purple hats and smiles wide,
They dance in breezes, full of pride.

The monkeys giggle, take a swing,
As petals rustle, birds will sing.
A kingdom built on nature's glee,
Where every whim's a jubilee.

Luminous Blooms of Joy

In daylight's glow, they strike a pose,
Winking at bees and funny toes.
With silly shapes that twist and turn,
Each bloom knows how to make us yearn.

The chef walks by, then stops and sighs,
With dreams of chips and bright blue skies.
In vivid tales, they share their flair,
A party waiting, wild and rare.

Soliloquy of Sweetness and Light

A chatter underneath the sun,
These vibrant blooms are having fun.
They whisper secrets in the breeze,
As elephants stomp, do what they please.

With candy sweetness in disguise,
They charm the bugs and thrill the flies.
In every nook, they share their cheer,
Their joy spreads wide from ear to ear.

Embracing Flora's Gentle Gift

A gift wrapped up in colors bright,
Makes everyone feel just so right.
With petals soft and laughter loud,
They sparkle like a jovial crowd.

In gardens lush where humor lies,
They tango under sunny skies.
Their playful twirl's a sight to see,
Their fun's a gift for you and me.

A Serenade for the Swaying Trees

In the garden, they do dance,
With a whimsy and a chance.
Petals prance on breezy days,
Leaves whisper gossip in their ways.

They giggle when the sun shines bright,
Bowing low, what a sight!
Swinging like a playful kite,
Nature's jesters, pure delight.

Every hum from buzzing bees,
Brings laughter among the trees.
A tickle here, a hug over there,
Nature's humor everywhere!

So join the fun, let worries cease,
In the sway, find your peace.
With flowers twirling, hand in hand,
Life's a joke in this lush land.

Blossoms that Touch the Soul

Petals peep with cheeky glee,
Hiding secrets, oh so free.
In the garden's lively stir,
Each bloom chuckles, what a blur!

With colors bright, they compete,
For the title of funniest treat.
Their jokes may be a little nutty,
But savoring them? Oh, how lucky!

The sun drips laughter on their heads,
Tickling dreams as daylight spreads.
With every breath, a fresh punchline,
In the garden where antics align.

Join the circus of vivid sights,
Where each sprout ignites delights.
Their humor is a fragrant muse,
In this realm of joyful views.

Secrets of the Garden's Heart

In the shade, a secret's told,
Of mischief made, of stories bold.
The blooms wear smiles, sneaky and sly,
As critters giggle, zooming by.

With every rustle of the leaves,
Nature spins tales and mischief weaves.
Petal parties go past the moon,
As blossoms chuckle out of tune.

Underneath the big green hat,
Grows a punchline, imagine that!
A tease from roots to tips of bloom,
Laughter echoes through the gloom.

So lend an ear to leafy jokes,
Where petals whisper, tree trunks poke.
In this garden's witty embrace,
Life's a dance, a charming chase.

Nature's Sweetest Intrigue

Oh, the game of hide and seek,
Where petals flutter, plants are chic.
Secrets swirl on gentle breeze,
Whispers exchanged among the leaves.

Giggles bounce on every vine,
Nature's jesters, oh so fine.
Blooming tales of joy untold,
In the sunlight, watch them unfold.

The garden holds a merry crew,
With cheeky plans for me and you.
Their laughter lingers in the air,
Filling hearts, a cosmic dare.

So skip along in roots and greens,
To join the fun behind the scenes.
With every chuckle, bloom, or nod,
Find the joy that nature's trod.

Elegy for Living Colors

In gardens bright, a sight awakes,
Petals giggle, give and take.
A yellow crown with swagger bold,
Stories of laughter, yet untold.

Beneath the sun, they twist and sway,
Embracing joy in their own way.
A riddle wrapped in leaves so fine,
Nature's jest, a playful sign.

Dance of the Luminescent Crown

A party starts when blooms unite,
With silly hats, oh what a sight!
They shiver, shake, and dance around,
In a carnival of colors found.

Twisting high as breezes blow,
A flutter here, a swish down low.
They laugh at bees who buzz in fright,
And wink at kids who gaze in delight.

Echoes of Earth's Silent Secrets

Whispers of green, a giggle's grace,
In secret nooks, they find their space.
Soft chuckles echo through the trees,
    Carried by the playful breeze.

They hide from those who seek them out,
In mysteries wrapped, of that no doubt.
The world's a jest and they partake,
    In colors bright, for laughter's sake.

Threads of Life in Gentle Curves

Spinning tales in a playful loom,
Each twist and turn could light a room.
Golden arcs in sunlight play,
Happy dancers in a vibrant sway.

Once mere buds hugged by the ground,
They rise to greet the joy around.
In every curve, a jolly jest,
Life's sweetest secrets, they express.

Blossom and Fruit: A Timeless Tale

In a garden where laughter grows,
A flower wears a yellow snout,
It giggles as the breeze blows,
Whispers sweet secrets, no doubt.

With petals soft as whipped cream,
It dances under the moon's gleam,
A fruit near the base does beam,
Together they form a silly team.

Bumblebees come by for a tease,
They hum and swirl with cheeky ease,
Oh what a sight, oh what a breeze,
A fruity flower sure to please!

As night falls, they share a sigh,
Dreaming of clouds that float by,
Who knew flowers could be so spry?
Let's eat, let's play, oh my oh my!

Tropical Dreams Unfurled

Underneath a sunny sphere,
A proud bud spreads its leafy cheer,
With laughter, it whispers, "Come here!",
As fruits giggle, filled with good cheer.

The birds swing by, their beaks aglow,
They tease the petals, swaying low,
"What's for lunch?" they chirp and crow,
"Something sweet? We'd surely know!"

Silly monkeys swing with flair,
Hitching a ride through the fragrant air,
"A jester's cap!" they shout in dare,
"Life's a party, we just don't care!"

Sunshine leads the way to fun,
Where petals and fruits play and run,
In a tropical world, everyone,
Dancing together, never done!

When Flowers Meet the Sun

Sunbeams tickle every bloom,
In a lively, sunny room,
Chasing shadows, banishing gloom,
With giggles that cause quite a boom.

A flower sports a playful hat,
While fruits roll 'round like a cat,
"Let's play tag!" they squeal and spat,
A cheerful world, imagine that!

Butterflies join with flapping wings,
Twisting and turning, oh, what it brings!
They laugh as gentle breezes sing,
In this frolic, joy's the king!

With each sunset, they share a toast,
To laughter and fun, we love the most,
For in this garden, we all boast,
Eternal joy, it's what we host!

Threads of Sunlight and Shade

In a patch where mischief weaves,
A cheeky flower plays with leaves,
It hides beneath while sunlight grieves,
Sharing stories that it believes.

Fruits wiggle and giggle in glee,
"Watch us dance! Come join the spree!",
As shadows blend with light so free,
Life's a circus, let's not flee!

Laughter hints at every turn,
Lessons in joy we all must learn,
Each petal gleams, each fruit will yearn,
In this paradise, bright hearts burn.

As day ends, they snuggle tight,
Tales of warmth fill the night,
In their dreams, they take flight,
Happiness blooms, pure delight!

The Whisper of Tropical Blooms

In jungles where the monkeys swing,
Petals giggle, and the toucans sing.
A purple crown atop a green sigh,
Made me wonder, oh me, oh my!

Bees hover with a buzzing tune,
Chasing nectar 'neath the bright moon.
Laughter drips from the leafy vines,
As nature playfully intertwines.

A curious sight, a wonderfully odd,
With fruits that look like they might nod.
In the shadows, critters exchange a glance,
As vibrant petals join the dance.

These funny blooms in tropical glee,
Whisper secrets to you and me.
If laughter's a flower, let it unfold,
In hues so bright, in stories told.

Sun-Kissed Floral Mysteries

Beneath the sun's warm, cheerful rays,
Flowers tease in flamboyant ways.
Petal hats on a bright green stalk,
Make cackles bloom with each soft talk.

A wiggly bug dons a suit so fine,
Giggling at the suns' bright shine.
Tiny friends in a floral house,
Tiptoeing with grace like a little mouse.

Oftentimes I stop and stare,
At flowers that flaunt without a care.
Colorful jokes in a garden fair,
Drawing smiles from folks everywhere.

Mysterious blooms with antics galore,
In gardens where laughter is never a chore.
Shared among buds, a chorus so bold,
Stories unfold as they shimmer in gold.

When Green Turns to Gold

In a world where green thumbs play,
Leaves chatter in a mischievous way.
The garden giggles with whispers shared,
As colors burst, mildly dared.

Transforming hues from vibrant green,
To golden sheens that gleam and preen.
Nature's jokesters, zany and spry,
Planting smiles as the hours fly by.

Each fruit a riddle, a puzzle to find,
With silly hats, they're one of a kind.
They hide and seek in the leafy maze,
Creating moments that endlessly amaze.

As laughter ripens, the colors unfold,
A story of sunshine, bright and bold.
When green turns to gold in playful jest,
Nature's magic passes its colorful test.

Nature's Fruitful Embrace

In nature's arms, a funny scene,
A floral hug that's soft and keen.
Petals giggling in playful delight,
In the daylight, oh, what a sight!

With cheeky blooms that blush and sway,
They dance around like kids at play.
Each vibrant face a joke to tell,
In this garden where laughter dwells.

Sweet scents mingle with mischief's roar,
As nature whispers, "Let's explore!"
Every petal's a shy little tease,
Tickling noses in the gentle breeze.

In this embrace, where fun is the goal,
Floral laughter fills up the soul.
A quirky paradise, a joyous chase,
In the heart of nature's playful grace.

Vibrant Echoes in the Air

In the tropical breeze, they sway,
Hiding giggles in their display.
Nature's laughter, a secret tune,
Dancing under the warm afternoon.

Petals draped like a fancy gown,
Whispering softly, never a frown.
They beckon bees with a cheerful shout,
Playing hide and seek, there's no doubt.

Silly shapes in a fluttering show,
Jokes to the sun, in a golden glow.
They tickle the air, a playful tease,
Bringing smiles like a sweet summer breeze.

Underneath their grand ballet,
They conspire to brighten the day.
In this garden, laughter is king,
As petals prance and the birds all sing.

Arrivals of Elegance

With royal caps on their heads so wide,
They enter the garden, full of pride.
Swirling in colors, oh what a sight,
Dressed to impress, they giggle in light.

Waving their skirts, they spin and twirl,
Who needs a crown when you can swirl?
Adventures await in each fragile fold,
Whispers of secrets and stories untold.

Ladies in waiting, poised and grand,
Shaking their petals like a cool band.
From the tropics, they come with flair,
A raucous welcome fills the air.

They sip on sunshine, dressed so bright,
Swaying and laughing with pure delight.
In this frolic, elegance plays,
With a wink and a nod, they dance all day.

Tropic's Hidden Treasures

In the jungle, a treasure chest,
With leafy wings, they do their best.
Golden jewels hug the stem tight,
Hiding away, out of sight.

A playful breeze makes them sway,
Chasing shadows that run away.
Laughter echoes in this green vault,
With every bloom, there's no fault.

Stripes and dots, such a fun mix,
Creating art with their leafy tricks.
Each petal a game of peek-a-boo,
Treasure awaits, come out and view!

In the heart of the lush, they shine,
Gathering stories, oh so divine.
Tropic's laughter spills all around,
In their gentle grip, joy is found.

The Bloom That Seeks the Sky

With a wink to the clouds, they rise,
Stretching their arms, chasing the skies.
They giggle at leaves that hang around,
Bouncing to the rhythm of nature's sound.

Their petals like laughter, bright and bold,
Telling secrets the sun told.
Reaching for dreams, they sway with glee,
As butterflies join in their spree.

They tickle the wind with fruity delight,
Turning the day into playful night.
Climbing higher, they spin and dangle,
In a twist of joy, they gently wrangle.

These cheeky blooms hold stories untold,
In their vibrant folds, adventure unfolds.
As they giggle with each sunny ray,
They play their part in the grand ballet.

Veils of Gold in the Green

In a jungle of laughter, so bright,
Hanging dreams dance in morning light.
Petals giggle, swaying with glee,
Nature's joke, just for you and me.

With a yellow smile, so wide and bold,
In the leafy troves, secrets unfold.
They tickle the breeze with a playful sigh,
As the sun winks back from the azure sky.

Fluffy creatures halt, heads held high,
Pointing at wonders as they float by.
They laugh at the weirdness, the silliness here,
As flowers juggle with joy, spreading cheer.

In this wacky green space, who can resist?
The petals perform, like a joyous twist.
With each swipe of color, a grin takes bloom,
Amidst nature's canvas, we cheer in the room.

A Whisper Among the Leaves

In a leafy world, secrets chuckle,
Where blooms play hide-and-seek in a shuffle.
Petals murmur jokes, oh what a sound,
A giggle so sweet, in green they abound.

Up high in the trees, the birds join in,
Chirpy laughter fills the air, a merry din.
The flowers blush red, with a tease in their eyes,
As they wink at the world in a colorful guise.

A breeze swoops low, and carries the tune,
Spreading whispers of joy beneath the bright moon.
The colors collide like a chaotic fun,
As nature throws a party, oh what a run!

In this whimsical land where giggles reside,
Leaves tumble together, no need to hide.
Every petal's a storyteller, swirling about,
In a cheeky ballet, they dance and shout.

Painting Moments in Vibrant Hues

Dipped in sunshine and splashed with glee,
Each colorful bloom tells a story, you see.
With a comical twist, they sway and they bend,
In this verdant gallery, laughter won't end.

Colors collide in a messy embrace,
Who knew nature could have such a face?
A paintbrush of whimsy splatters the ground,
Creating a chuckle where mirth can be found.

The artist weaves shadows under the sun,
Where each leaf can giggle and have so much fun.
These wild strokes of nature know no bounds,
As petals burst forth in hilarious sounds.

With a twist of the stem and a flick of a leaf,
Nature's own laughter brings joy and relief.
In this garden of humor, just look and see,
A canvas of chuckles, forever carefree.

The Story of a Sun-Kissed Bloom

Once upon a time, in a sunlit spree,
A bloom caught a sunbeam, as lively as can be.
It caught the giggles of the tiny ants,
Who lined up to share their funny little chants.

The petals pranced, with a wink at the sun,
"Guess I'm the star of this botanical fun!"
With every bright ray, it danced and it spun,
In a comedic ballet, where everybody's won.

"Oh look at me!" cried a petal so proud,
"I'm the best yellow joke in this cheerful crowd!"
While leaves clapped their hands, with a rustle and cheer,
As the stories of laughter drifted from ear to ear.

Each day brought adventure, with giggles galore,
In this realm of color, who could ask for more?
So here's to the laughter and the sun's golden light,
Where every bloom tells a tale that feels just right.

Soft Sighs of the Jungle

In the thick green, a munching sound,
Monkeys swing low, jumping around.
Trying to reach, what's high and bright,
A dance of delight, in the warm sunlight.

Bees are buzzing with happy glee,
Pollinating with tea, or was it brie?
They wear tiny goggles, sunglasses askew,
Planning parties, in the leafy view.

Colors splatter the jungle floor,
A feast of oddities, never a bore.
Listen closely, the wild things squeak,
As nature plays hide-and-seek!

With each puff of breeze, the laughter flows,
While creatures prance in whimsical rows.
In this realm, the silly reigns,
A jungle joy, with no refrains.

The Poetry of Nature's Gifts

In the midst of big, broad leaves,
Tiny critters plot, what one believes.
With a wiggle and a giggle, they sway and spin,
Sharing secrets of mischief, where to begin?

The sun plays checkers with shadows around,
While ants march in lines, without a sound.
Carrying treasures, a sweet surprise,
Wondering if it's lunch or fun in disguise.

Laughter breaks as frogs play their tune,
Croaking loud under the lazy moon.
Each ribbit a joke, they're the comedians here,
Spreading the joy, with no room for fear.

When petals fall like confetti from above,
It's clear the jungle is in love.
With joyous sounds, they fill the air,
Nature's laughter—beyond compare.

Lush Echoes of the Tropics

In the jungle, there's a party scene,
With ferns in hats, feeling quite keen.
Dancing sloths take it nice and slow,
While cheeky birds put on a show.

Fruits hang out in a vibrant array,
While the trees nod along to the play.
Giggling vines twirl and sway,
As if to say, it's a fun-filled day!

A friendly lizard gives a wink,
With a silly grin that makes one think.
Creating mischief in the thick green hue,
Oh, what a site, the wild crew!

When night falls, the stars twinkle cheer,
Nature's partygoers, with no fear.
In this wild space, laughter springs,
Echoing joy, the jungle sings!

Nectar-Laden Whispers

Beneath leafy shadows, giggles abound,
As bees gossip about the best candy found.
They buzz round flowers, slipping and sliding,
A sweet comedy show, oh, how they're gliding!

Chirping crickets plan a grand affair,
In a symphony where fun fills the air.
Each chirp a punchline, no time for frowns,
They wear their finest, no room for clowns.

An echidna stumbles, then strikes a pose,
Declares to the crowd, "Look at my clothes!"
Spines all in style, it's a new trend,
Nature's fashion, it seems to transcend!

In this tapestry of laughter and cheer,
The whispers of joy ring loud and clear.
Through petals and leaves, this bliss is spun,
In nature's embrace, the last laugh is won.

Cradled by Nature's Soft Touch

In a garden lush and bright,
Petals sway with pure delight,
Bouncing blobs in hues so grand,
Swinging gently, hand in hand.

Silly shapes that tickle the eye,
They wave hello as I walk by,
With wiggly strands that twist and twirl,
Nature's humor starts to unfurl.

Tiny creatures start to dance,
In the shadows, they prance and prance,
A jester's cap, or could it be,
A flower's hat, so wild and free?

Oh, what a sight, a splendid scene,
Where laughter reigns and joy is keen,
In this cradle, full of cheer,
Nature's giggle is ever near.

A Journey through the Lush Canopy

On a quest through leafy dreams,
A canopy with silly schemes,
Fronds like fingers wave and shout,
Join the fun, there's no doubt!

Bouncing blooms, in shades of glee,
Laughing down at little me,
A guide who never stays in line,
Each twist and turn, a jest divine.

Whispers soft, the trees conspire,
Joking roots that never tire,
With petals giggling in the sun,
My journey's laughter has begun.

A rustle here, a chuckle there,
Floral antics fill the air,
These playful sights, they never stop,
In nature's play, I'm on the hop!

Fables of Floral Delight

Gather 'round, let tales be spun,
About the blooms that love to run,
With quirky tops and goofy forms,
They weather all the brightest storms.

Once there was a flower so bold,
It wore a coat of yellow gold,
With petals shaped like smiling lips,
It danced on breezes, took funny trips.

A curious bee with buzzing grace,
Could never keep a straight-faced pace,
It tumbled, fumbled, oh what sight,
In fields of joy, pure delight!

So listen close, as life unfurls,
In every bud, a tale twirls,
A fable rich with laughter's light,
Amongst the vibrant blooms so bright.

Blush of Nature's Bounty

A blush of colors, oh what fun,
Nature's harvest, playful run,
Floral faces, cheeks aglow,
Wink and giggle, steal the show!

Dressed in gowns of leafy green,
These cheeky blooms, a lively scene,
They strike a pose, flash a smile,
Turning every head for a while.

Beneath the sun, they spin and sway,
With laughter bright, they greet the day,
A troupe of buds, in playful zest,
Sharing joy, they are the best!

So when you stroll through gardens fair,
Look for the grins hiding there,
For in each petal, laughter's found,
In nature's bounty, joy is crowned.

Flowering Secrets of the Tropics

In the jungle, a joke takes flight,
Petals giggle, what a sight!
With a wink and a sway, they tease the air,
Nature's punchline, blooming without care.

Pollinators zoom with buzzing glee,
Dressed in stripes, they dance free.
They laugh at the blooms, a floral show,
"Come join us, it's all about the glow!"

A bright umbrella hides a funny face,
Chasing butterflies in a wild race.
Leafy giggles, oh what a scene,
Tropical humor, forever keen!

In the sun's warm embrace, they sway,
A floral carnival, come what may.
With petals like laughter, they spread the cheer,
Tales of the tropics, we all hold dear.

Golden Petals in Sunlight

Golden petals shine like silly hats,
Wobbling gently, where the monkey chats.
They wave to the ants on a comedic trip,
"Join the party, just don't slip!"

Sunbeams tickle the leaves alive,
Where blossoms twirl, and critters dive.
A parade of color, what a fun plot,
The quirkiest garden, like it or not!

Chasing shadows, they play peek-a-boo,
With each flutter, a giggle ensues.
Flowers teasing, with a cheeky grin,
"What's the punchline? Let the fun begin!"

So blooming bright, they whisper and cheer,
With the laughter of nature, we draw near.
In the sunlight's glow, nonsense prevails,
Golden petals spin their whimsical tales!

Unraveling the Veils of Flora

With layers of petticoats, who knew?
These blooms play dress-up, it's true!
Veils of laughter as they prance about,
Unraveling secrets, laughing out loud.

Each blush of color tells a joke,
As bees buzz in with a little poke.
"What's the best flower? You'll just have to see!"
Flora's giggles echo, wild and free.

The sun throws a party, come take a look,
A fruit-fueled dinner, not in a cookbook.
Leafy friends join with a hearty cheer,
Revealing the fun that's lurking here!

With petals unfurling, mischief begins,
In this floral circus, everyone wins!
In the tapestry of green, joy abounds,
Nature's comedy where fun surrounds.

The Dance of Tropical Dreams

In a dance-off under the blazing rays,
Petals flutter, in brilliant arrays.
With laughter and twirls, a sight so grand,
Tropical dreams do a funky handstand.

With fruit hats on their leafy heads,
They shimmy and shake on vibrant beds.
"Who said flowers can't bust a move?"
Join in the rhythm; it's time to groove!

Crickets play music, the frogs clap along,
A concert of colors, where all belong.
With a flip and a flop, they jive in delight,
In this gala of greens, everything feels right!

So sway like a blossom, let laughter bloom,
In the tropical hall where joy finds room.
Let's dance 'til the sun dips low,
In dreams of petals, let the good times flow!

The Music of Summer's Heart

In a garden with something so bright,
The petals dance in the warm sunlight.
Bumblebees buzzing, they wear a grin,
As petals giggle and sway in the din.

A fruit that's a trumpet, how wild the sound,
With notes that tumble, oh, round and round.
Each twist is a song, each turn is a beat,
The roots tap along to the rhythm so sweet.

The leaves hold secrets of laughter and cheer,
In summer's embrace, all worries disappear.
They chuckle with breezes that tickle the air,
While critters join in without a care.

So let's raise a tune, let joy take a flight,
Where blue skies are laughter and days are so bright!
In the rhythm of life, we dance in the park,
With music that echoes from morning till dark.

The Enchantment of Tropical Flora

In the jungle, where creatures prance,
There's a flower with a curious stance.
With petals that jive and giggle on cue,
It paints the world in a funny hue.

Like hats on a parade, they flit and they sway,
In colors so bright, they brighten the day.
A wink from the sun, and they all erupt,
As critters conspire, and laughter erupts.

The vines twist in jest, what a tangled affair,
As the ants put on shoes and dance without care.
Each creature's a dancer with steps oh so fine,
While flowers clap petals, keeping time just divine.

Oh, the charm of the bloom in its playful spree,
With nature's own laughter, so wild and so free.
Let's spin with the colors, let's laugh with delight,
For enchantment's alive in the tropical light.

Secrets Beneath the Exotic Canopy

Underneath the leafy green veil,
Where whispers of mischief begin to sail.
The critters convene for a jovial feast,
With laughter that bounces, it's not for the least.

The petals are giggling, oh what a sight!
They play peek-a-boo 'neath the moon's gentle light.
Secrets exchanged in a language so sweet,
As the roots tell tales of the latest new beet.

The shadows are filled with a curious tease,
Where lizards join in, bending their knees.
And each little flower with stories to share,
Beneath this grand canopy, joy fills the air.

So come take a stroll through this musky old lane,
Where laughter and secrets mingle like rain.
In nature's embrace, we find our delight,
With stories of whimsy that dance through the night.

Fertile Hues of Joy

In a garden where giggles bloom bright,
Colors explode in a glorious sight.
The petals are chuckling, it's quite a parade,
As bees buzz and dance to the songs that they've played.

With hues of delight, the world wears a grin,
Each blossom a smile that draws you all in.
The leaves are conspirators, tickling the breeze,
While vines play hopscotch with the curious trees.

Every twist and every turn sparkles with fun,
As sunlight paints pictures, a dance just begun.
With fruits just a-winking, all charmingly bold,
Their laughter ignites stories waiting to unfold.

So pluck out your worries; let joy take the stage,
In a world bursting with whimsy, let's scribble a page.
With the fertile hues of a jolly delight,
Let's dance with the blooms, from morning till night.

Tropical Shades and Fragrant Dreams

In the shade of leaves that sway,
A flower's hat goes out to play.
It giggles soft in breezy curls,
Like a dance with twirling pearls.

Bumblebees wear tiny shoes,
Inviting all to share their views.
They sip the nectar, oh so sweet,
While petals chuckle at their feet.

Laughter's found in every fold,
As colors burst, their stories told.
Like clowns who paint the skies anew,
In nature's circus, there's a view!

When fruit falls down and starts to roll,
It leads the way, a merry stroll.
With cheeks so bright and grins so wide,
The party starts, come on, let's ride!

The Elegance of Embers

A crimson crown atop so bold,
It winks at all the tales untold.
With every breeze, it spills some glee,
A filters of elegance, can't you see?

In garden circles, it takes the prize,
Waving to friends under sunny skies.
It fluffs its leaves, strikes a pose,
And giggles softly as color flows.

Each petal whispers secrets dear,
To butterflies that linger near.
With every rustle, laughter bright,
Bringing joy from morn till night.

As dusk begins to steal the show,
Twinkling stars begin to glow.
But mystery lingers in the air,
As the flower spins, a funny affair!

A Tapestry Woven in Green

In a tapestry where colors blend,
A laughing bloom wishes to send.
It prances high on leafy scales,
Like a creature with storytelling tails.

Round its edges, mischief plays,
Swirling in the heat of rays.
With every sway, it paints a grin,
An artist's gift where fun begins.

In parties held beneath the sun,
Where insects come to dance and run,
With graceful moves and haughty flair,
The flower twirls, none can compare!

With festive shades and joyful tunes,
It celebrates the afternoon,
Beneath the sky, laughter flows,
In whimsical joy, this beauty grows!

Hues of Happiness in the Sun

In golden light, a splash of cheer,
Where petals laugh and dance near.
They sway like dancers in a line,
In every color, they brightly shine.

With silly shapes and funny hats,
They grace the garden, play with cats.
Their rhymes are filled with goofy sounds,
As giggles and smiles abound.

Around them swirls a lively crew,
With bees and birds who join the flue.
They make a ruckus, sing aloud,
Turning heads, they're oh so proud!

And when the sun begins to fade,
The flower winks, the laughter stays.
In hues of joy, the day concludes,
With memories made in funny moods!

Nectar of the Earth

In the jungle, a flower once spry,
A shady deal, I can't deny.
Bees buzz in, with nectar so sweet,
Waltzing in time, they shuffle their feet.

It sways with laughter, quite a tease,
Winking at creatures, dancing the breeze.
A feast for the critters, a fragrant delight,
Who knew blooms could party all night?

Frogs in tuxedos hop to the show,
While ants serve snacks, in rows, they go.
With petals flamboyant, they cheer and prance,
In their floral fiesta, they jig and dance.

So here's to the laughter, the colors and flair,
Nature's own jesters, beyond compare.
Next time you wander where the wild things roam,
Join in the fun, you're welcome to come!

Blossoms of Dusk and Dawn

At dusk they giggle, at dawn they blush,
In sunshine and shadows, they love to rush.
A playful dance from morn till night,
With winks and chuckles, what a sight!

They peek at the sky with a gleeful grin,
As butterflies twirl, they all join in.
The sun tickles petals, like kids on a spree,
Oh, what a spectacle, come dance with me!

With laughter they rustle, in the soft, warm air,
Creating a ruckus, without any care.
A carnival shining, in bright, silly hues,
In this floral chaos, you'll not lose your shoes!

So if you find joy where the wild things play,
Remember those blooms who brighten the day.
With petals like party hats, they surely know,
How to bring giggles wherever they grow!

Whispered Hues of the Rainforest

In the realm of green, where whispers roam,
A flower's giggle is calling you home.
With colors that chuckle and shapes that grin,
They tickle the senses, oh let the fun begin!

Mischief they sow in their leafy abode,
Playing hide and seek on their vibrant road.
As critters convene for a whimsical feast,
It's a laugh-tastic gathering, to say the least!

The jungle's a courtroom, with petals as jurors,
Judging the jokers, those playful explorers.
They gather their gossip, giggling with glee,
A mock-serious tone, do you hear that decree?

So waltz through the blossom, let joy take a chance,
In this leafy extravaganza, come join the dance.
With whispers of fun, in the tropical air,
You'll find laughter and joy, beyond compare!

A Symphony of Yellow and Green

In the concert of green, there's a bright spotlight,
Where petals compose a comical sight.
A symphony soaring, with each little breeze,
As nature's jesters hum tunes with such ease.

Yo, leaves on the trees, join in the refrain,
With cackles from critters, in harmony they gain.
A slapstick ballet, as they twirl and spin,
The colors all mingle, where fun begins!

Caterpillars croon their smooth little verse,
While ladybugs strut, like a one-lady purse.
The rhythm is catchy, a playful delight,
As the flowers sway gently, from morning till night.

So listen intently to nature's grand show,
Where yellow and green put on quite a flow.
With laughter and smiles spilling out like confetti,
In this vibrant spectacle, you're sure to be ready!

A Dance of Yellow and Green

In the garden, they sway and twirl,
With petals that spin, a vibrant whirl.
They giggle and laugh as they dress up bright,
A party of colors, a pure delight.

Like dancers in hats that are large and round,
They sway to the rhythm of the wind's sound.
A feast for the eyes, in this sunny scene,
Who knew that veggies could be so keen?

The chef's in trouble, just can't pick one,
With flavors so wild, it's a tasty fun.
They cheer in the sun, as if on the stage,
Each one a character, full of sweet rage.

So here's to the blooms, so funny and grand,
Dressed up for a feast, not a single bland.
Join the dance, let your laughter ring,
With these vibrant wonders, let the joy spring!

The Hidden Blooms of Paradise

In secret corners of leafy greens,
A hidden joy, like silly scenes.
They giggle as they hide from the bees,
Hoping to evade their sticky squeeze.

Peeking out shyly, they blush with flair,
Winking at sunbugs that flutter in air.
They're masters of trickery, oh what a sight,
Disguised as decor, but fully in flight.

With each gentle breeze, they quirk and sway,
Making the butterflies stop and play.
"What's that?" asks the ladybug, grinning wide,
"It's a giggly show; come join the ride!"

So wander the garden, discover their game,
These cheeky blooms without any shame.
Their laughter's contagious, their humor bright,
In hidden spots, they spread pure delight.

Sweet Curves of the Tropics

With shapes so silly, they curve and bend,
Making the fruit flies laugh and pretend.
Sunny and cheeky, they dance in the breeze,
Their sweetness is juicy, sure to please.

They twist like a dancer, with flair and style,
Drawing us in with a cheeky smile.
"Dare you to munch us," they call with glee,
"We're packed with joy, come see what we be!"

In tropical light, they play hide and seek,
Making folks giggle, no words need to speak.
With every sweet curve, they whisper a cheer,
"Life's a big party, come join us here!"

So lift up your spirits, it's time to munch,
On funny little fruits, if you dare to crunch.
With sweet tropic wonders, life's full of fun,
In the world of delights, the day's just begun!

Harvesting Dreams from the Tree

Gather 'round friends, there's fun to be had,
In the land of green, where dreams aren't sad.
With a hop and a skip, we reach for the sky,
Those wacky delights, oh my, oh my!

Climbing the trees, we giggle with grace,
Each fruit a treasure, a funny embrace.
They dangle and tease, like a riddle to solve,
With whimsical shapes that love to revolve.

"Catch me if you can!" one playfully shouts,
As we leap and we reach, full of fun sprout doubts.
We gather the dreams from branches so wide,
With laughter and joy, in the sunshine we bide.

So let's harvest the giggles, every kind,
In the orchard of laughter, true joy we find.
With sweet dreams in bag, we dance and we weave,
In the tree of delight, it's hard to believe!

Curves of Life's Abundance

In the garden, they sway and sway,
With shapes that brighten the dullest day.
Nature's frill in a vibrant hue,
Whispers secrets only they knew.

With laughter tucked in every fold,
Stories of sweetness waiting to unfold.
They giggle softly in the breeze,
Tickling the bees with such sweet ease.

They wear their skirts with such flair,
Dancing and twirling without a care.
A party hosted by nature's own,
Where joy and silliness proudly shone.

On sunny days, they love to tease,
Making the bumblebees laugh with ease.
Life's abundance wrapped in green,
In their playful realm, joy is seen.

Harvesting the Sunshine

In fields so bright, they wave like flags,
With sunny smiles that never drag.
They hoard the laughter, sweet and true,
Harvesting joy with a vibrant hue.

With petals soft like temperamental hats,
They flirt with the whims of curious cats.
A brunch of laughter on every morn,
In the dance of life, they are reborn.

Sipping sunlight is their favorite sport,
Turning mundane moments to a joyful court.
They twirl with breezes, sing sweet tunes,
Under the gaze of benevolent moons.

Their jests are ripe, like fruit in the sun,
Making every mundane moment fun.
A sweet serenade from the green brigade,
In the garden's laughter, memories made.

Gentle Hands of the Blossom

With tender grips of leafy hands,
They cradle dreams like grains of sands.
Telling tales without a word,
In a language that's seldom heard.

Their soft embrace a silly thing,
As giggles flutter with the spring.
Twirling round like dizzying spins,
Catching the whispers of breezy grins.

Oh, the mischief they surely sow,
As they wave at clouds and put on a show.
In their velvety touch, joy's cradled tight,
Lighting up shadows, chasing away night.

With a wink and nod, they dance in glee,
Inviting all critters to share the spree.
With gentle humor and hearts so grand,
Creating smiles all over the land.

The Language of Softest Petals

In the chat of leaves, secrets exchange,
With petals soft, funny and strange.
Conversations drifting through the air,
Silly stories with a lively flair.

Like cushions where laughter takes a seat,
They gather chuckles, oh so sweet.
Every breeze whispers jokes galore,
Nature's comedy, that we adore.

With colors that tickle the wise and bold,
They melt away worries, laughter unfolds.
A tapestry of joy, braided with light,
In their playful charm, everything feels right.

So here's to the giggles found all around,
In the garden's embrace, where fun can be found.
They teach us to dance, to sing, and to play,
In the language of petals, brightening our day.

When Nature Paints in Yellow

In gardens bright, a curious sight,
Petals dangling, a floral delight.
They sway and giggle in the breeze,
Nature's prank, aiming to tease.

With every puff, they catch a cheer,
Bright yellow suits, so bold, so sheer.
Buzzing bees in a playful dance,
Around these wonders, they skip and prance.

A banquet set for the critter crew,
Sticky fingers suspicious, who knew?
Laughter spills from bee to bough,
As nature giggles, just look at how!

In the sun, they shine and beam,
A funny twist to nature's theme.
With every bloom, a chuckle flows,
In the garden, where humor grows.

The Allure of the Tropic Shade

Beneath the leaves, a secret fair,
Where flowers flaunt without a care.
They wear their hats, all frilly and grand,
In a hush of green, they take a stand.

Whispers of color, how they tease,
With winks and nudges from playful bees.
The sun plays tag, in hues of gold,
While laughter in petals, a story told.

Sipping nectar, the critters dine,
Delighted sighs, oh how they shine!
These little wonders in laughter stowed,
Under the shade, where joy is sowed.

Slipping and sliding, the bugs all chase,
Their rosy cheeks in a floral race.
Amidst this greenery, giggles resound,
In nature's theater, great fun is found.

Dappled Light on Exotic Blooms

In patches of light, the colors unfold,
With splashes of laughter, bright and bold.
Exotic wonders, they twist and twirl,
In a carnival dance, they give it a whirl.

Sunshine winks through foliage green,
A zany parade, quite the scene.
Each petal's a shout, in hues so bright,
Making shadows giggle in dappled light.

Flitting and fluttering, the butterflies play,
In this lively show, they're here to stay.
With whimsical gowns, they take to the sky,
A joyful ballet, oh me, oh my!

Lively banter with each friendly buzz,
A medley of fun, just because.
In this vibrant realm, where laughter blooms,
Nature's silly jokes, oh how it looms!

Fruitful Reveries of the Canopy

Up in the trees, a tale's to weave,
With fruity dreams that dance and cleave.
A canopy chorus, a vibrant tune,
In the theater of leaves, beneath the moon.

Colorful antics, oh what a scene,
Where each hanging fruit is fit for a queen.
Swinging and swaying, oh what a sight,
Nature's punchlines, take flight tonight!

With cheeky birds, who mimic and chime,
They giggle along, keeping perfect time.
These jewels of the forest, so merry and bright,
Beckoning all to join in their flight.

So lift your spirits, come dance with glee,
In this joyful world, wild and free.
Each fruity whimsy, a cause for delight,
In the canopy's embrace, we'll party all night!

Bathed in Nature's Gentle Glow

A flower hangs like a silly hat,
In the garden where the critters chat.
It sways with pride, oh look at me!
Just a fancy petal on a leafy spree.

Bees buzz around like they lost their keys,
Dancing circles, trying to tease.
With nectar sweet like candy dreams,
Not a worry, just sunshine beams.

The petals giggle in a mellow breeze,
Waving to the ants with utmost ease.
Tiny creatures join the fun,
In this flowery party under the sun.

As twilight falls, the stars peek through,
The giggling petals bid adieu.
With moonlight lending sweet serenades,
Nature's jesters in leafy parades.

Colors of Abundance

Orange, yellow, a rainbow sigh,
A burst of laughter in the sky.
Shapes of joy, like a balloon,
Hanging out with the bees' afternoon.

Each swirly petal, a spinning top,
Giggling at the raindrops that plop.
Ready to dance when the sun comes bright,
In this garden, pure delight!

Wiggly vines play tag with leaves,
As playful birds gather and weave.
Colors splashing all around,
In this happy place where joy is found.

The sun dips low, the day's finale,
Silly shadows begin to rally.
Like kids at dusk, they jump and play,
In a patch of color, they stay.

Flourishing in Sunlight's Embrace

Stretching leaves as wide as smiles,
In a sunny nook, they've bloomed in style.
Giggling with the fluttering bees,
Sipping sunshine, breezy teas.

With each ray, they throw a dance,
A twirl and swirl, oh, what a prance!
Like laughing children, blossoms cheer,
Bright and vibrant, full of cheer.

When clouds roll in, they don't despair,
They put on frowns, a funny fair.
"Oh no, the sun has gone away!"
Yet, together they giggle and play.

As evening drapes its curtain low,
The blooms whisper sweet hello.
In petals soft, a laughter rests,
A garden full of sunny jest.

The Symphony of Tropical Flora

In the jungle, a concert brews,
With flowers jiving, singing their blues.
Petals clap and vines do sway,
Nature's rhythm, come join the fray!

The palm leaves rustle a breezy tune,
While the critters dance under the moon.
Each plop of fruit, a drumbeat there,
Creating laughter in fragrant air.

With colors that giggle under the sun,
They tickle the eye, oh what fun!
Each bloom a note in this merry choir,
Sending waves of joy that never tire.

As twilight kisses the verdant scene,
The blossoms wink, oh, what a dream!
In a joyful symphony, they nestle tight,
A tropical jamboree, pure delight.

The Enchantment of Golden Layers

In the garden, they sway, oh so bright,
Dressed in yellow, a comical sight.
With a wink and a nod, they tease the sky,
Whispers of laughter as bumblebees fly.

Dancing in the breeze with a giggly flair,
Each layer unfolds, revealing the rare.
Sticky fingers reaching for dreams above,
Like playful kittens, they purr and shove.

Sunny hats on their heads, oh what joy!
Cheeky and charming, they never annoy.
If plants could chuckle, they'd burst at the seams,
In a world made of whimsy, they reign supreme!

What secrets they keep in their golden folds,
With each giggle shared, a story unfolds.
In this whimsical realm, no frowns to trace,
Just joy and mischief in the sun's warm embrace.

Sentinels of the Rain-kissed Grove.

Guardians of giggles in a lush green mask,
With layers of laughter, they love to bask.
Wet from the rain, they chuckle and sway,
Looking for trouble in their playful way.

Draped in mystery with a cheeky grin,
Each petal like a jest, where mischief begins.
They tease the rain, swaying to and fro,
With puddles to splash, oh what a show!

Wiggling their edges like playful gnomes,
These merry sentinels never feel alone.
A chorus of chuckles echoed through the trees,
As they play host to the wandering breeze.

In laughter and joy, they take their stand,
A riot of giggles in this vibrant land.
With nature's own jesters, they frolic and sing,
Turning the grove into a whimsical thing.

Golden Petals in the Breeze

Fluttering softly, like laughter in flight,
Golden petals dance, oh what a delight!
In the warm sunlight, they wink and they wave,
Each pirouette playful, a sight to save.

Chasing the wind with a mischievous air,
Spinning and twirling without a care.
They flippity-flop, with a giggle so sweet,
Lighting up the garden, a whimsical treat.

Like tiny sunbeams, they play hide and seek,
All the while chatting, oh, the fun they speak!
In the land of the vibrant, where whimsy prevails,
Their chuckles echo through the meadows and trails.

Gather 'round folks, for a jolly old time,
As golden petals lift our spirits to climb.
In this dance of delight, let your worries cease,
For in nature's funny ballad, there's only peace.

Nature's Velvet Secrets

Soft like velvet, with secrets untold,
A tale of mischief wrapped tight in gold.
With a flap of their layers, they giggle and tease,
In this wild concert, they bow to please.

Hidden in greenery, they share their delight,
With whispers of fun that charm day and night.
They bloom with a smirk, oh what a surprise,
Each berry a jest that twinkles and flies.

In fungi-shaped chairs, they hold court with grace,
While the critters join in for a topsy-turvy race.
Nature's wild humor, unyielding and bright,
Bringing laughter to all in the soft moonlight.

So tread with a giggle through this velvet realm,
Where fun has no limit, and laughter's the helm.
Join the playful chorus, let worries be few,
For amidst the green laughter, there's always something new!

Essence of the Jungle's Heart

In a leafy crown, the clowns reside,
With vibrant hues that tickle and bide.
They sway and dance in silly glee,
A cheeky show of nature's spree.

Giggles burst from senorita's bloom,
Flapping like wings in a tiny room.
They jest and joke with sunny smiles,
While critters join in with their wiles.

A jester's hat with petals galore,
They caper and prance, calling for more.
Laughter echoes through the trees,
While breezy whispers make us tease.

So join the fun in this forest fair,
Where colorful antics charm the air.
A riot of colors, a playful art,
Essence found in the jungle's heart.

Floating Whispers of the Wild

In the thicket sings a silly sight,
With petals twirling in sheer delight.
They float on breezes, soft and sweet,
Tickling noses wherever they meet.

Hooting monkeys in a playful blend,
Join the jive, their antics suspend.
A gentle sway, a giggle's sound,
A floral frolic where laughs abound.

Whispers ride the winds of cheer,
As happy voices draw near.
In this dance of whispers bright,
Nature's jesters take their flight.

So lift your spirits, don't delay,
Join the revelry, come what may.
The wild sings out, a joyful tune,
In a world where laughter makes us swoon.

A Tapestry of Foliage and Flickering Light

A patchwork quilt of silly smiles,
With glowing petals stretching miles.
They twirl like dancers, bright and bold,
In nature's theater, tales unfold.

Swaying leaves in a comical jig,
Chasing shadows, oh so big!
Laughter blooms in every hue,
In this playful garden, joy is due.

A wink from the sun through branches play,
Brought to life in a zany way.
Colorful whispers on the breeze,
Will tickle your thoughts with teasing ease.

So strut along this leafy lane,
Let every petal share their reign.
In this whimsical, brightened plight,
Life's a tapestry of flickering light.

Metamorphosis of a Floral Vision

With a flip and a flop, they do emerge,
A transformation, a lively surge.
Petals in giggles, swaying shy,
While critters look on with a curious eye.

In playful puffs of fluffy dreams,
The jungle bursts with sunny beams.
Laughter bubbles at the sight,
Of flowers dressed for a funny night.

Shapes and forms that twist and bend,
A riot of joy that will not end.
Embracing quirks, flowing free,
A merry twist in harmony.

So let the petals take their chance,
To jig and jiggle in nature's dance.
From buds to blooms in a cheery spin,
A metamorphosis where fun begins.

The Art of Blooming Richly

In a garden where oddities reign,
Petals dance like they've lost their brain.
Wobbling stems in a dizzy display,
Who knew flowers could frolic this way?

With colors that giggle and twist in the air,
They bounce like they're caught in a silly affair.
Forget all the rules, they refuse to comply,
Such artistry makes the bees laugh and sigh.

Like parties of colors throwing a laugh,
Creating a scene of pure floral gaff.
Who needs a canvas when blooms do exist?
The whims of the petals surely can't be missed!

So tiptoe through gardens where humor's the trend,
And let the lush blooms be your most quirky friend.
For in every flourish and flap they proclaim,
Life without laughter is really quite lame.

Petals of Joy in the Mist

Through morning mist, where antics are rife,
Flora prances with the joy of life.
Leaves giggle softly, the dew drops tease,
As curls of petals sway with ease.

With a splash of humor in every hue,
They joke with the sun, as they stretch and skew.
Look! A flower's pose that could make you chuckle,
Dressed down in bold shades with flair and snuggle.

In a twist here and a twirl there,
Sprouting silly looks, flowers declare,
"Join the fun, revel in our cheer,
We bloom to laugh, not live in fear!"

Their laughter echoes, a floral dance,
With each little petal, you have a chance.
So embrace the joy, let your spirit play,
In the mist of petals, life's a bouquet!

Where Flora Meets the Sky

Up where the sunshine flirts with the blue,
Blooms hold a contest of whimsical view.
Spinning and swaying, they crack witty jokes,
As butterflies giggle and tumble in strokes.

The sky's not the limit, it's merely the start,
With foliage making their own kind of art.
"Look at me, I'm taller," they boast with a grin,
While clouds scribble laughter, somewhere within.

In this playful realm, the colors collide,
With hues that are quirky and beams that glide.
Bees in tuxedos, all polished and prim,
Join in the fun, with a sylvan hymn.

So fly with the blooms that bring life to the air,
Nature's own jesters with silliness rare.
For where flowers meet the vast open sky,
Laughter's the secret – come join and fly!

Vibrant Hearts of the Jungle

In the heart of the jungle, where vibrance reigns,
Flora is jiving without any chains.
With giggles wrapped in green leafy wraps,
They whisper wild secrets and silly mishaps.

Colors leap forward, making a scene,
Like cartoons in bloom, they dance and they preen.
Petals like party hats tip to the breeze,
Encouraging laughter among playful trees.

"Who's the fairest?" they question, adorned in delight,
With shenanigans blossoming day and night.
An audience of monkeys tunes in to the fun,
Each blossom a punchline, said under the sun!

So venture with joy into this jungle spree,
Where vibrant hearts bloom, wild and free.
For in every petal, a chuckle awaits,
Nature's own comedy, as laughter creates!

Nature's Pendant of Gold

In a garden where laughter reigns,
A silly fruit with bright yellow stains.
Hanging upside down, what a sight!
It giggles in the sunshine, pure delight.

A crown of purple, a jester's flair,
Swinging on stems, swaying in air.
It waves to the bees, a quirky parade,
In this fruity circus, no plans ever made.

One day it dreamed of being a hat,
For a squirrel who loved his acrobat.
With a toss and a twirl, the wind gave a tease,
Now it's just a roly-poly breeze.

The laughter of nature, a jest so sweet,
In the land of oddities, where fun and fruit meet.
So join this fiesta, without a care,
And dance with the blossoms, if you dare!

Rustic Beauty in Soft Unfurling

In the countryside, odd shapes do bloom,
A floppy hat, a whimsical loom.
"Oh my!" chirps the sparrow with glee,
"What is this wonder hanging from the tree?"

Each petal unfurls with a silly grin,
Mocking the sun while soaking in sin.
Rustic charm with a punny twist,
Like a sitcom flower you can't resist!

The farmer looks up, scratching his head,
"Is this a fruit or a dance for the dead?"
With giggles and wiggles, it plays a tune,
A folly of nature beneath the moon.

So grab your hats and join the dance,
With each petal flapping, it takes a chance.
In fields of laughter where silliness springs,
The rustic beauty wears joy on its wings!

Lush Dreams Drifting on the Breeze

A whimsical cloud that found its way,
Drifting on breezes, come join the play!
Lush green laughter that floats with mirth,
Whispering secrets beneath the earth.

In gardens where dreamers find delight,
A fruity giggle hides out of sight.
With petals unfurling, a joy to share,
Dancing in sunlight, like magic in air.

"Hey there!" it calls to the buzzing bees,
"Let's throw a party, come join with ease!"
In bloom it teases, with scent oh so bright,
As colorful dreams take wing in the light.

So let us imagine, let's lose all care,
For lushness abounds in this colorful air.
With each little laugh and giggle we find,
A breezy adventure that's joyfully kind!

The Cascading Crown of Soft Petals

Look up, look up, at the crown on the vine,
A joyful display, so silly, divine.
A cascade of colors, a splash of glee,
It's a royal comedy hanging from tree!

With soft petals twirling in merry delight,
It tickles the skies, a whimsical sight.
"Join me for tea!" it calls to the breeze,
"Bring your wild friends and bend your knees!"

"Who needs a tiara?" it chuckles with mirth,
"When petals can wear the crown of the earth?"
Wobbling and bobbling, a fanciful show,
A cascade of crown jewels that dance in a row.

So gather around for a jolly good time,
With crowns made of laughter, each petal a rhyme.
In this comical garden where joy takes its seat,
We'll dance in the petals, a playful retreat!

www.ingramcontent.com/pod-product-compliance
Lightning Source LLC
Chambersburg PA
CBHW051733290426
43661CB00123B/261

9781805862406